I0407570

THE HUNDRED DOLLAR HUSTLE

BLUEPRINT FOR A PROFITABLE BUSINESS

Rodney T Harris II

Copyright © 2023 Rodney T Harris II

All rights reserved

The characters and events portrayed in this book are fictitious. Any similarity to real persons, living or dead, is coincidental and not intended by the author.

No part of this book may be reproduced, or stored in a retrieval system, or transmitted in any form or by any means, electronic, mechanical, photocopying, recording, or otherwise, without express written permission of the publisher.

ISBN: 9798860740648

Printed in the United States of America

CONTENTS

Title Page

Copyright

The Hundred-Dollar Hustle: Blueprint for a Profitable   1
Business

Chapter 1: The $100 Challenge   3

Chapter 2: Finding Your Profitable Idea   7

Chapter 3: Market Research on a Tight Budget   13

Chapter 4: Building a Lean Business Plan   18

Chapter 5: The Art of Cost Cutting   24

Chapter 6: Innovative Funding Strategies   30

Chapter 7: DIY Branding and Marketing   34

Chapter 8: Sales Strategies on a Tight Budget   40

Chapter 9: Customer Relationship Building   46

Chapter 10. Scaling Up with Profits   52

Chapter 11. Overcoming Common Challenges   59

Chapter 12: Building a Sustainable Business   65

Chapter 13: Financial Management for a $100 hustle   70

THE HUNDRED-DOLLAR HUSTLE: BLUEPRINT FOR A PROFITABLE BUSINESS

Introduction: The Hundred-Dollar Hustle - Your Path to Become Profitable

In entrepreneurship, it's easy to get swept away by tales of million-dollar investments, Silicon Valley success stories, and colossal business valuations. While these stories capture our imaginations and inspire dreams, they often overshadow a remarkable truth: some of the most outstanding businesses began with little more than a dream and a mere $100.

Welcome to "The Hundred-Dollar Hustle: Blueprint for a Profitable Business," a journey into entrepreneurial possibilities on a tight budget. Suppose you've ever felt that your lack of capital was the sole barrier to launching your business. In that case, this book dispels that notion and empowers you to take your entrepreneurial aspirations to new heights.

As we embark on this journey together, we'll explore the art of starting a business from scratch, armed with only $100. We'll delve into the world of bootstrapping, where every penny counts, and we'll discover innovative ways to fund your venture when necessary. We'll learn how to craft a lean yet effective business plan tailored to your budget and adapt marketing and branding strategies to make a lasting impression without breaking the bank.

While we'll explore the practical aspects of launching a low-budget business, "The Hundred-Dollar Hustle" is more than just a manual for aspiring entrepreneurs. It's a roadmap to turning dreams into reality, proving that the seeds of entrepreneurship can grow even in the most unlikely soil.

So, this book is your compass whether you're a businessperson with a hundred-dollar bill and a vision or someone waiting for the right moment to take that leap of faith. It's your guide to navigating the twists and turns of building a profitable business on a budget.

Let's begin the Hundred-Dollar Hustle together and unleash the entrepreneur in you.

CHAPTER 1: THE $100 CHALLENGE

Unlocking the Potential: Ideas to Turn Your Hundred into More

In entrepreneurship, there's a common misconception that substantial capital is a prerequisite for success. It's easy to be overshadowed by stories of massive investments and multimillion-dollar deals. Yet, beneath the surface lies an unexplored path—one where a mere $100 bill can begin your entrepreneurial journey.

The Significance of $100

Hold that $100 bill in your hand for a moment. While it may appear modest compared to the financial juggernauts of the business world, it has the incredible potential to fuel your dreams and ignite your entrepreneurial spirit.

The Unique Challenge

Starting a business with just $100 presents a challenge unlike any other. It compels you to rethink the conventional notions of entrepreneurship. While limitations certainly exist, they can also become the breeding ground for innovation, resourcefulness, and creativity.

The Lean Approach

Before we dive into the possibilities that a $100 budget

can unlock, let's introduce you to the concept of the lean approach. Rooted in efficiency, this methodology champions resourcefulness, experimentation, and adaptation.

Validating Your Vision

A cornerstone of the lean approach is the art of validating your business concept before committing significant resources. With a modest $100 budget, this validation process becomes essential. It ensures you're not squandering your limited funds on an unproven idea.

Continuous Learning and Adaptation

Learning from setbacks is par for the course in the unpredictable terrain of entrepreneurship. With limited resources, you'll learn and adapt rapidly, reducing the cost of errors. This iterative approach empowers you to refine your business model, tweak your product or service offerings, and enhance customer interactions based on real-world feedback.

Agility and Speed

The lean approach values agility and swiftness as strategic assets. Traditional business models often entail extensive planning that consumes valuable resources. In contrast, the lean methodology encourages swift action, adjustments based on data and feedback, and a culture of rapid iteration. This approach aligns seamlessly with the constraints of a $100 budget, allowing you to pivot as needed without exhausting your initial investment.

Ideas to Multiply Your $100

Now that we've established the potential of your $100 bill and the principles of the lean approach, let's explore various innovative ideas to help you grow your initial investment into something substantial.

The Micro Niche E-Store

Identify a particular and underserved niche in the e-commerce landscape. Invest in a small quantity of niche products that cater to a dedicated audience. Use social media and online marketplaces to connect with your target customers.

The Freelance Strategy

Leverage your $100 to build a personal brand as a freelancer. Invest in a professional website and use your funds to learn new skills or tools in high demand. As you complete projects and gain experience, your earning potential will increase.

The Content Creator

Create valuable content in a niche you're passionate about, and as your audience grows, monetize through advertising, sponsorships, or affiliate marketing. All you need is a cell phone to start.

The Local Service Provider

Consider starting a service-based business, such as lawn care, pet sitting, or house cleaning. Use your $100 to purchase necessary supplies and market your services locally. Word-of-mouth referrals can be a powerful asset in this type of business.

The Digital Product Creator

Craft digital products like e-books, online courses, or digital artwork. Once created, these products can be sold repeatedly, offering a scalable income source.

The Reseller

Identify profitable products and sources where you can acquire items at a discount. Use your $100 to purchase a small inventory and set up shop online, whether on online marketplaces or through your website.

Embarking on Your $100 Challenge

With the potential of your $100 bill established and a range of ideas to consider, it's time to initiate your entrepreneurial journey. The path ahead may present challenges, but it's in overcoming these challenges that you'll discover your most incredible opportunities.

As we dive deeper into this book, we'll provide practical guidance and actionable steps to help you transform your $100 investment into a thriving business. Each chapter will bring you closer to your goal, equipping you with the knowledge and confidence to navigate entrepreneurship's exciting yet challenging terrain.

CHAPTER 2: FINDING YOUR PROFITABLE IDEA

Tips for Brainstorming and Selecting a Business Concept That Work

In the journey from $100 to a profitable business, one of your initial and most critical steps is finding the right business idea. This chapter is all about igniting your creativity, guiding your thought process, and helping you select a concept that excites you and holds the potential for success.

The Power of a Profitable Idea

A profitable business begins with a promising idea. It's the foundation upon which you'll build your venture, and finding a concept that resonates with you and your target audience is essential.

Your Unique Perspective

Your journey starts with exploring your unique perspective, skills, and passions. Often, the most successful business ideas stem from the intersection of what you love, what you're good at, and what the market needs. Ask yourself:

- What are your hobbies and interests?
- What skills or expertise do you possess?
- Are there any problems you've encountered that

you're passionate about solving?

Market Research

To ensure your idea has potential, conducting thorough market research is crucial. This doesn't require a large budget; it demands your time, effort, and curiosity. Look into:

- Who your target audience is, and what their needs are.
- Your competitors and what sets your idea apart.
- Current market trends and emerging opportunities.

Tips for Brainstorming

Now, let's talk about the art of brainstorming. Generating ideas is a creative process that can lead to breakthroughs. Here are some strategies to stimulate your creativity:

Mind Mapping

Start with a central concept or word related to your interests or skills. Branch out with related ideas, subtopics, and keywords. Mind mapping helps you visualize connections and uncover potential business ideas.

Problem-Solving

Think about common problems people face and consider how you can provide solutions. Often, businesses are born out of addressing pain points.

Cross-Pollination

Explore industries or niches that may seem unrelated to your background. Sometimes, innovation occurs when you combine ideas from different fields.

Trendspotting

Stay updated with industry news, emerging trends, and changes in consumer behavior. Identifying trends can lead to timely and profitable business ideas.

Idea Journal

Keep a journal or digital document to record every idea, whether small or insignificant. Over time, you may discover patterns or refine your concepts.

Idea Validation

Once you've generated several potential business ideas, it's time to validate them. You want to ensure that your concept has the potential to meet demand and create profits.

Feasibility Analysis

Evaluate the feasibility of each idea. Consider the required resources, market size, competition, and your capabilities.

Prototype or MVP

Creating a prototype or minimum viable product (MVP) for specific ideas can be invaluable. An MVP allows you to test the waters with a basic version of your product or service.

Surveys and Feedback

Gather input from potential customers or your target audience. Surveys and focus groups can provide valuable insights into the appeal of your idea.

Cost-Benefit Analysis

Estimate the costs associated with launching and running your business idea. Compare these costs to the potential revenue and profitability.

Narrowing Down Your Options

As you validate your ideas, some will shine brighter than others. It's time to narrow your options and choose the statement that resonates most with you and aligns with your resources and goals.

Passion and Commitment

Consider your passion and commitment to the idea. Building a business can be demanding, and your enthusiasm will be a driving force.

Market Potential

Evaluate the market potential of each idea. Are there customers willing to pay for your product or service? Is there room for growth?

Competitive Advantage

Assess the competitive landscape. What sets your idea apart from existing solutions or competitors? A unique selling proposition can be a significant advantage.

Scalability

Think about the scalability of your idea. Can it grow over time, or will it remain limited in scope? Scalable businesses have the potential for long-term success.

The Chosen Idea

Once you've selected your business concept, it's time to move forward with enthusiasm and determination. Remember that your chosen idea is just the beginning; the real work lies ahead as you transform it into a profitable venture.

Your Idea in Action

In the chapters, we'll guide you through the practical steps of bringing your idea to life. You'll learn how to create a business plan, acquire the necessary resources, and develop a strategy for success.

Continuous Learning

Embrace a mindset of continuous learning. Your idea may evolve, and your business will encounter challenges. Adaptation and education will be your allies in the journey.

Taking the First Step

The path from $100 to profitability begins with finding

the right idea. Now that you've chosen your concept, it's time to take that critical first step. Your entrepreneurial adventure awaits.

CHAPTER 3: MARKET RESEARCH ON A TIGHT BUDGET

How to Gather Valuable Market Insights Without Spending Much

Market research is the compass that guides your business decisions. Understanding your target audience, competition, and industry trends is essential for success. However, you don't need a substantial budget to gain valuable insights. In this chapter, we'll explore cost-effective methods to conduct market research on a tight budget.

The Importance of Market Research

Before diving into budget-friendly methods, let's reiterate the significance of market research for your business:

1. Understanding Your Audience

Market research helps you define and understand your target audience. Who are your potential customers? What are their needs, preferences, and pain points? With this knowledge, you can tailor your products or services to meet their demands effectively.

2. Evaluating Competition

Analyzing your competitors is crucial. What are their

strengths and weaknesses? How can your business differentiate itself? Market research provides insights into your competitive landscape, allowing you to position your venture strategically.

3. Identifying Trends

Staying informed about industry trends and developments is essential for adaptation and innovation. Market research keeps you up to date with emerging opportunities and challenges.

Budget-Friendly Market Research Techniques

Let's explore cost-effective strategies for gathering valuable market insights:

1. Online Surveys

Online surveys are an accessible and affordable way to collect data from your target audience. Numerous survey platforms offer free or low-cost options. Create surveys with questions relevant to your business goals and distribute them through email, social media, or your website.

Tips for Effective Online Surveys:

- Keep surveys concise and focused.
- Use multiple-choice and scaled questions for easy analysis.
- Incentivize participation with small rewards or discounts.

2. Competitor Analysis

Study your competitors to understand their strategies and identify gaps you can fill. Explore their websites, social media profiles, and customer reviews.

3. Online Forums and Communities

Participate in online forums and communities related to your industry or niche. Engage in discussions, answer questions, and observe conversations to understand your target audience better.

4. Customer Interviews

Conducting one-on-one interviews with potential customers can provide invaluable qualitative insights. Reach out to your network or use social media to find willing participants. Interviews can be given over the phone, through video calls, or in person.

Tips for Effective Customer Interviews:

- Prepare open-ended questions to encourage detailed responses.
- Listen actively and ask follow-up questions to dive deeper into responses.
- Record interviews or take detailed notes for analysis.

5. Crowdsourcing Feedback

Leverage the power of crowdsourcing for products or services. Crowdfunding platforms often feature comment sections where potential backers provide feedback and suggestions.

6. Google Trends

Google Trends is a free tool that provides insights into search volume trends over time. It can help you identify rising or declining interest in specific keywords or topics related to your industry. Use this information to adjust your content and marketing strategies accordingly.

7. Library Research

Don't underestimate the value of library resources for in-depth industry research. Many libraries provide free access to market research reports, industry journals, and academic papers. Explore their databases and archives to gather comprehensive insights.

8. DIY Website Analytics

Install free website analytics tools like Google Analytics to monitor your website's performance. Analyze data on visitor demographics, behavior, and traffic sources. This information can help you refine your online presence and content strategy.

9. Public Data Sources

Explore publicly available data sources such as government websites, census data, and industry associations. These sources can provide valuable demographic, economic, and market data specific to your region or industry.

Analyzing and Applying Your Findings

Gathering data is just the first step; analyzing and applying your findings is equally crucial:

Data Analysis

- Organize and analyze the data you've collected systematically.
- Look for patterns, trends, and key takeaways.
- Identify actionable insights that can guide your business decisions.

Pivot and Adapt

- Use your research to refine your business strategy.
- Make informed decisions about product development, marketing, and customer engagement.
- Be prepared to pivot based on emerging insights and changing market conditions.

Continuous Research

Market research is an ongoing process. Stay vigilant and continue to gather insights as your business evolves. Consumer preferences, industry trends, and competitive landscapes change over time.

Conclusion

Market research doesn't require a hefty budget. With creativity, determination, and the right tools, you can gather valuable insights to inform your business's growth. Your commitment to understanding your target audience, industry trends, and competition will drive your business's success.

CHAPTER 4: BUILDING A LEAN BUSINESS PLAN

Crafting a Business Plan Tailored to Your Budget and Goals with $100

In the journey from $100 to a profitable business, a well-crafted business plan can be your roadmap to success. While traditional business plans often involve extensive research, financial projections, and comprehensive strategies, as a budget-conscious entrepreneur, you can create a lean business plan that focuses on crucial essentials without breaking the bank.

The Role of a Lean Business Plan

A lean business plan is a condensed version of a traditional business plan. It's designed to provide clear direction, outline goals, and establish the fundamentals of your business without the need for elaborate details. Here's why it's essential:

1. Clarity of Vision

A lean business plan forces you to define your business's core purpose, target audience, and unique value proposition. It helps you clarify your vision and ensures that you and your team are on the same page.

2. Goal Setting

Setting clear and achievable goals is critical to any business's success. A lean business plan helps you define measurable objectives, such as revenue targets, customer acquisition goals, or product development milestones.

3. Resource Allocation

With a limited budget of $100, allocating your resources wisely is crucial. A lean business plan helps you outline your budget, identify essential expenses, and prioritize spending to achieve your goals.

4. Adaptability

In the dynamic world of startups, adaptability is vital. A flexible, lean business plan allows you to adjust your strategies and goals as you learn from your experiences and gather new insights.

Components of a Lean Business Plan

1. Executive Summary

- Concisely describe your business, its mission, and your primary goals.
- Provide an overview of your products or services and your target audience.
- Highlight your unique selling proposition (USP) and the problem you're solving.

2. Business Description

- Explain your business idea in more detail.
- Outline the market need or problem your

business addresses.

• Describe your vision for the business's future.

3. Market Analysis

• Summarize your market research findings, emphasizing key insights.

• Identify your target audience and their demographics, needs, and preferences.

• Provide a brief analysis of your competitors and how your business stands out.

4. Marketing and Sales Strategies

• Outline your marketing strategies, considering your budget constraints.

• Describe your sales channels and customer acquisition tactics.

• Emphasize how you plan to reach and engage with your target audience effectively.

5. Product or Service Offering

• Detail your product or service offerings.

• Explain how your offerings meet customer needs and provide value.

• Highlight any unique features or advantages.

6. Budget and Financial Projections

• Create a budget that outlines your expected income and expenses.

• Specify how you plan to allocate your $100 budget.

• Provide simplified financial projections,

including revenue estimates and expense forecasts.

7. Action Plan and Milestones

• Outline specific actions you'll take to achieve your goals.

• Set clear milestones and deadlines for each action.

• Highlight the most critical steps required to move your business forward.

8. Team and Roles

• If applicable, list your team members and their roles.

• Emphasize their relevant skills and contributions.

• Describe any gaps in your team that you plan to fill.

9. Risks and Mitigations

• Identify potential risks or challenges your business may face.

• Describe strategies or contingencies you'll employ to mitigate these risks.

• Show that you've considered possible obstacles and have plans to overcome them.

10. Measurement and Evaluation

• Define key performance indicators (KPIs) to track your business's progress.

• Explain how you'll measure success and evaluate the effectiveness of your strategies.

• Indicate how often you'll review and adjust your plan based on your measurements.

The Lean Business Plan in Action

As you craft your lean business plan with a budget of $100, keep in mind that simplicity and clarity are your allies. Focus on the most critical aspects of your business and how you'll achieve your initial goals.

Here's a sample scenario to demonstrate how your lean business plan can work:

Scenario: Starting a Freelance Writing Service

Executive Summary: We aim to provide high-quality content writing services to small businesses looking to enhance their online presence.

Business Description: Our business will offer blog post writing, website content creation, and social media copywriting services.

Market Analysis: Small businesses need help to maintain consistent online content. There's a demand for affordable, professional writing services.

Marketing and Sales Strategies: We'll use social media marketing, content marketing, and email outreach to connect with potential clients. Our website will serve as our primary sales channel.

Product or Service Offering: We'll offer three writing packages tailored to different business needs.

Budget and Financial Projections: With a budget of $100, we'll allocate $40 for website hosting and $60 for initial marketing efforts. We project to earn $1,000 in revenue within the first three months.

Action Plan and Milestones: In the first month, we'll launch our website and start marketing. By the second month, we aim to secure our first client. In the third month, we'll focus on client retention and scaling.

Team and Roles: The business will be a one-person operation, handling all writing and marketing tasks.

Risks and Mitigations: Potential risks include difficulty acquiring clients and intense competition. We'll offer competitive pricing and emphasize our unique value to mitigate this.

Measurement and Evaluation: Key metrics include website traffic, conversion rates, and client retention. We'll review our plan monthly and adjust our strategies based on performance.

Conclusion

A lean business plan tailored to your budget of $100 provides the foundation for your business success. It distills your vision, goals, and strategies into a concise roadmap. As you take the following steps in your entrepreneurial journey, remember that your plan is a living document that can adapt and evolve as your business grows. Stay focused and use your lean business plan as a compass to guide you toward profitability.

CHAPTER 5: THE ART OF COST CUTTING

Strategies for Cutting Costs and Making the Most of Your Resources

In the journey from $100 to a profitable business, one of the most crucial skills you'll need is cutting costs effectively. Managing your limited resources wisely can be the difference between survival and success. This chapter explores the art of cost-cutting and offers strategies to maximize your financial efficiency.

The Significance of Cost Cutting

Why is cost-cutting so critical, especially when starting with a small budget? Here's why:

1. Resource Optimization

Cost cutting ensures you optimize your limited resources, allowing you to allocate funds where they matter most. It's about getting the most value out of every dollar you spend.

2. Financial Sustainability

Savvy cost management extends your financial runway, providing more time to grow your business and generate revenue. Without effective cost control, you might run out of funds prematurely.

3. Competitive Advantage

Efficient operations can lead to competitive pricing, making your products or services more appealing to customers. You can offer competitive prices while maintaining healthy profit margins by keeping your costs down.

4. Adaptability

In the dynamic world of business, adaptability is critical. A lean financial approach allows you to pivot and adapt to changing market conditions and unexpected challenges. It gives you the agility needed to thrive in uncertain environments.

Cost Cutting Strategies

Let's dive into the strategies that will empower you to cut costs without sacrificing quality or growth potential:

1. Prioritize Expenses

Identify essential expenses that directly contribute to your business's growth and profitability. These could include marketing, product development, or customer acquisition costs. Prioritize these expenses and allocate your budget accordingly. Not all prices are equal, and some investments are necessary for long-term success.

2. Negotiate

Negotiation is a valuable skill for any entrepreneur. When dealing with suppliers, service providers, or contractors, explore opportunities for negotiation. Seek discounts, bulk purchase deals, or favorable payment terms. Vendors often appreciate long-term relationships and may be willing to negotiate for your business.

3. Embrace Digital Tools

Leverage digital tools and technology to streamline operations and reduce costs. Consider cloud-based software for accounting, project management, and communication. These tools often offer cost-effective solutions for small businesses. Automating repetitive tasks can free up time and resources for more critical activities.

4. Outsourcing and Freelancing

Instead of hiring full-time employees, explore outsourcing or freelancing options for specific tasks. Freelancers can provide specialized services without the overhead costs of permanent staff. It's a flexible arrangement that allows you to scale up or down as needed.

5. Optimize Marketing Efforts

Invest in cost-effective digital marketing strategies. Focus on content marketing, social media, and email marketing to reach your target audience without the need for extensive advertising budgets. Track the performance of your marketing campaigns to refine your strategies over time. Digital marketing platforms often provide detailed analytics to help you measure your ROI (Return on Investment).

6. Inventory Management

If your business involves physical products, efficient inventory management is crucial. Avoid overstocking by using inventory tracking systems. This ensures that capital is maintained in excess inventory. Similarly, minimize the risk of stockouts by monitoring demand and replenishing stock strategically. Over time, this practice can lead to significant cost savings.

7. Lean Business Processes

Implement lean business processes to eliminate waste and reduce inefficiencies. Conduct regular process audits to identify areas where improvements can be made. Streamline workflows, reduce unnecessary steps, and standardize procedures wherever possible. Encourage employees to contribute ideas for process improvements, as they often have valuable insights into day-to-day operations.

8. DIY When Feasible

Consider taking on tasks yourself if you have the skills and time. Whether it's website maintenance, content creation, or basic bookkeeping, handling certain aspects of your business can save money. However, be mindful of your strengths and weaknesses. While DIY can be cost-effective, it's essential to recognize when delegating specific tasks to experts is more efficient.

9. Vendor Evaluation

Regularly assess your vendors and suppliers to ensure

you're getting the best value for your money. Don't hesitate to switch suppliers if you find better alternatives. Evaluate factors such as quality, reliability, pricing, and customer service. Building strong vendor relationships can also lead to favorable terms and discounts.

Continual Cost Monitoring

Cost-cutting is an ongoing process. It's crucial to continually monitor and assess your expenses, making adjustments as needed. Regularly review your financial statements, budgets, and cash flow projections to maintain your financial health. Set aside time each month or quarter to analyze your expenditures and identify areas for further savings.

The Art of Balance

While cost-cutting is essential, it's equally important to strike a balance. Avoid overly aggressive cost-cutting measures that compromise product quality, customer service, or employee morale. Remember that some investments are necessary for future growth. Prioritize cost-cutting actions that have the most negligible impact on your core business functions and customer experience.

Conclusion

Cost-cutting is a fundamental skill for every entrepreneur, especially when starting with a modest budget. By implementing intelligent cost-cutting strategies, you'll optimize your resources, increase your financial sustainability, and position your business for long-term success. It's not just about spending less; it's about spending smarter. Mastering the art of cost-cutting will empower you to make the most of your limited resources and confidently navigate the challenging early stages of your business.

CHAPTER 6: INNOVATIVE FUNDING STRATEGIES

Creative Ways to Raise Additional Capital If Needed

In the journey from $100 to a profitable business, you might encounter situations where you need additional capital to fuel your growth. While traditional funding sources like loans and investors are familiar, this chapter explores creative and unconventional ways to raise money on a tight budget. From leveraging your skills to tapping into community resources, numerous innovative approaches to securing the funding you need exist.

1. Freelance Your Skills

Consider freelancing if you possess marketable skills such as writing, graphic design, coding, or digital marketing. The income from freelancing can be a valuable source of additional capital to invest in your business.

2. Crowdfunding Campaigns

Create compelling campaigns offering backers early access, exclusive perks, or limited edition products in exchange for financial support. A well-executed crowdfunding campaign can raise funds, generate buzz, and validate your business concept.

3. Affiliate Marketing

Explore affiliate marketing programs related to your niche or industry. Promote products or services through your website or social media channels and earn a commission for each sale generated through your unique affiliate link. With strategic marketing, affiliate income can grow over time and provide steady funds.

4. Leverage the Gig Economy

The gig economy offers opportunities for short-term and freelance work. Consider participating in gig platforms such as TaskRabbit, Uber, or DoorDash to earn extra income that can be directed toward your business. It's a flexible way to raise funds without a significant upfront investment.

5.. Barter and Trade

Explore barter and trade arrangements with other businesses or individuals. If you offer a product or service that can benefit another party, consider exchanging your offerings for goods or services you need. Bartering can help you conserve cash while obtaining valuable resources.

6.Grants and Competitions

Research grants, awards, and business competitions related to your industry. Many organizations and government agencies offer funding opportunities for innovative businesses. While competition for assistance can be fierce, winning one can provide a significant financial boost.

7. Local Business Grants and Programs

Explore local business development grants and programs offered by your city or region. Some local governments provide financial incentives, tax breaks, or grants to support small businesses contributing to the local economy.

8. Host Fundraising Events

Organize fundraising events within your community or online. Events like charity auctions, virtual galas, or crowdfunding campaigns can raise funds while generating goodwill and support from your network.

9. Partner with Complementary Businesses

Collaborate with businesses that complement yours. Joint ventures or partnerships can lead to shared marketing efforts, reduced expenses, and additional funding sources. Identify companies that share your target audience and explore mutually beneficial arrangements.

10. Secure Vendor Financing

Negotiate favorable terms with your suppliers or vendors. Some suppliers may offer extended payment terms or financing options, allowing you to manage cash flow more effectively. This can be particularly beneficial for businesses with inventory or production needs.

Conclusion

Creativity and resourcefulness can be your greatest assets when securing additional capital in the entrepreneurial journey. These creative funding sources, whether freelancing your skills, launching crowdfunding campaigns, or forming strategic partnerships, offer viable avenues to raise funds and support your business's growth.

Remember that the key to successful fundraising is a compelling pitch, a well-thought-out plan for capital use, and a clear vision of how the additional funds will contribute to your business's success. Stay open to new opportunities, adapt to changing circumstances, and hustle for the capital you need to reach your business goals.

CHAPTER 7: DIY BRANDING AND MARKETING

Cost-effective Branding and Marketing Techniques for Startups

Effective branding and marketing play a pivotal role in the journey from $100 to a profitable business. However, as a business with limited resources, you might wonder how to create a strong brand presence and reach your target audience without breaking the bank. This chapter explores cost-effective do-it-yourself (DIY) branding and marketing strategies to help you establish your brand and attract customers.

The Importance of Branding

Before diving into DIY branding and marketing techniques, it's essential to understand the significance of branding for your startup:

1. Brand Identity

Your brand identity is how the public perceives your business. It includes your logo, colors, fonts, and the overall visual elements representing your brand. A well-crafted brand identity creates a memorable and professional image.

2. Brand Trust

A strong brand instills trust and confidence in your potential customers. When they see a consistent and appealing brand, they will likely choose your products or services over competitors.

3. Differentiation

Effective branding sets you apart from the competition. It highlights what makes your business unique and why customers should choose you. In a crowded marketplace, differentiation is crucial.

4. Customer Loyalty

A well-defined brand builds customer loyalty. When customers connect with your brand on a deeper level, they're more likely to return for repeat business and become brand advocates.

DIY Branding Strategies

Let's explore cost-effective DIY branding strategies that will help you create a compelling brand identity:

1. Define Your Brand

Define your brand's values, mission, and unique selling proposition (USP). What does your business stand for, and how does it solve your customers' problems? These insights will guide your branding efforts.

2. Create a Memorable Logo

Your logo is a visual representation of your brand. You don't need to hire a designer; there are online logo makers and design tools that allow you to create professional-looking logos on your own.

3. Choose Brand Colors and Fonts

Consistency in color and font choices is vital to branding. Select colors and fonts that align with your brand's personality and message. Use these consistently across all your marketing materials.

4. Craft a Brand Story

Compellingly tell your brand's story. Share how your business started, what motivates you, and your journey. Authentic storytelling can resonate with customers and create emotional connections.

5. Design a Memorable Business Card

Business cards may seem old-fashioned, but they remain a powerful branding tool. Design a unique and memorable business card with your logo, contact information, and a brief tagline or value proposition.

6. Build a Professional Website

Your website is often the first point of contact for potential customers. Use website builders to create a professional and user-friendly site. Ensure that your branding elements are consistent across your website.

DIY Marketing Strategies

With your branding foundation in place, let's explore cost-effective DIY marketing strategies:

1. Content Marketing

Content is a powerful marketing tool. Create blog posts, articles, videos, or infographics that provide value to your target audience. Share your expertise and establish yourself as an industry authority.

2. Social Media Marketing

Leverage social media platforms to connect with your audience. Choose the platforms most relevant to your business and create engaging content. Consistency and authenticity are essential to social media success.

3. Email Marketing

Build an email list and regularly send out newsletters or updates to your subscribers. Email marketing is a cost-effective way to nurture leads and engage with your audience.

4. Search Engine Optimization (SEO)

Optimize your website for search engines to increase organic traffic. Conduct keyword research and create high-quality, relevant content that ranks well in search results.

5. Networking and Partnerships

Connect with other businesses, influencers, or organizations in your industry. Collaborative partnerships and networking can expand your reach and introduce your brand to new audiences.

6. Customer Reviews and Testimonials

Encourage satisfied customers to leave reviews and testimonials. Positive feedback builds trust and credibility, making it easier to attract new customers.

7. Guerrilla Marketing

Guerrilla marketing involves unconventional and low-cost tactics to promote your business. Examples printing off flyers from your home computer and handing them out in person.

8. Public Relations (PR)

Write press releases and reach out to local media outlets or industry publications. Getting featured in news articles or blogs can provide valuable exposure.

Measuring Your Branding and Marketing Efforts

To ensure your DIY branding and marketing efforts are effective, measuring their impact is crucial. Use analytics tools to track website traffic, social media engagement, email open rates, and other relevant metrics. Adjust your strategies based on the data to improve your results continually.

Conclusion

DIY branding and marketing strategies empower startups to build a strong brand presence and attract customers without significant financial investments. You can compete effectively in the marketplace by defining your brand, creating a memorable logo, and implementing cost-effective marketing techniques like content marketing, social media, and email marketing.

Consistency, authenticity, and a deep understanding of your target audience are essential to successful branding and marketing. As you implement these strategies, stay open to feedback, adapt to changing trends, and refine your approach to ensure your brand continues to evolve and thrive.

CHAPTER 8: SALES STRATEGIES ON A TIGHT BUDGET

Tactics for Generating Sales Without a Big Advertising Budget

In the journey from $100 to a profitable business, sales are the lifeblood of your business. However, allocating funds for extensive advertising campaigns is challenging when operating on a tight budget. This chapter explores effective sales strategies that won't drain your wallet. You can generate sales and drive revenue without a big advertising budget by focusing on resourcefulness and creativity.

The Value of Effective Sales

Before diving into the strategies, it's crucial to recognize the importance of effective sales techniques:

1. Revenue Generation

Sales are the primary source of revenue for your business. Consistent sales ensure a steady cash flow to cover expenses and invest in growth.

2. Customer Acquisition

Sales represent an opportunity to acquire new customers. Each sale is a chance to build relationships, gain customer trust, and potentially secure repeat business.

3. Business Growth

Successful sales strategies contribute to business growth. As you refine your sales processes and expand your customer base, your business can scale and thrive.

4. Brand Building

Effective sales can enhance your brand's reputation. Positive customer interactions and referrals contribute to brand recognition and trust.

Sales Strategies on a Tight Budget

Let's explore cost-effective sales strategies tailored for startups with limited advertising budgets:

1. Identify Your Ideal Customer

To maximize your sales efforts, define your ideal customer. Understanding their needs, preferences, and pain points allows you to tailor your messaging and offerings to resonate with them.

2. Create a Compelling Value Proposition

Craft a value proposition that communicates the unique benefits of your product or service. Highlight how it solves customers' problems or improves their lives.

3. Leverage Content Marketing

Content marketing isn't limited to branding; it can drive sales, too. Create informative blog posts, videos, or guides that showcase your expertise and subtly promote your offerings.

4. Optimize Your Website for Conversions

Your website is a powerful sales tool. Ensure it's user-friendly and optimized for conversions. Implement clear call-to-action buttons and provide easy ways for visitors to contact you or make a purchase.

5. Offer Limited-time Promotions

Create a sense of urgency by offering time-limited promotions or discounts. Limited-time offers encourage potential customers to take action quickly.

6. Harness the Power of Email Marketing

Email marketing remains a cost-effective way to nurture leads and convert them into customers. Build an email list and send targeted, value-packed emails that drive sales.

7. Encourage Referrals

Satisfied customers can be your best salespeople. Encourage referrals by offering incentives or rewards to customers who refer friends or family.

8. Networking and Partnerships

Connect with other businesses or entrepreneurs in your industry. Collaborative partnerships and networking can lead to joint sales efforts, expanding your customer reach.

9. Implement Upselling and Cross-selling

Once you have a customer's attention, maximize sales by offering related products or complementary services. Upselling and cross-selling can significantly increase the average transaction value.

10. Customer Follow-up

Don't neglect existing customers. Regularly follow up with personalized messages, special offers, or updates to encourage repeat purchases and build customer loyalty.

11. Use Social Proof

Highlight customer testimonials, reviews, and success stories on your website and marketing materials. Social proof can boost trust and confidence in your offerings.

12. Sales Funnel Optimization

Examine your sales funnel and identify areas for improvement. Streamline the process to reduce friction and make it easier for prospects to become customers.

13. Attend Trade Shows and Events

Participating in trade shows or industry events can provide valuable face-to-face interactions with potential customers. It's an opportunity to showcase your products or services and generate leads.

14. Leverage Influencer Marketing

Partner with micro-influencers or industry experts who

align with your brand. They can promote your products or services to their engaged audiences.

15. Cold Outreach

While often challenging, cold outreach can yield results. Reach out to potential customers via email, social media, or phone, focusing on personalized and value-driven messaging.

Measuring Your Sales Efforts

To ensure your sales strategies are effective, measuring their impact is essential. Use sales analytics tools to track key performance indicators (KPIs) such as conversion rates, sales funnel progression, and revenue generated through each strategy. Analyze the data to refine your sales tactics continually.

Conclusion

Sales strategies on a tight budget require ingenuity, persistence, and a deep understanding of your target audience. You can drive sales without a substantial advertising budget by identifying your ideal customer, creating compelling value propositions, and leveraging cost-effective tactics like content marketing, email marketing, and customer follow-up.

Remember that successful sales aren't solely about making transactions but building relationships and delivering value. As you implement these strategies, adapt to customer feedback, refine your approach, and stay committed to providing exceptional customer experiences.

CHAPTER 9: CUSTOMER RELATIONSHIP BUILDING

Cultivating Strong Customer Relationships for Repeat Business and Referrals

In the journey from $100 to a profitable business, your relationship with your customers is paramount. Building and nurturing strong customer relationships leads to repeat business and transforms satisfied customers into advocates who refer your products or services to others. This chapter delves into customer relationship building, offering strategies to create meaningful connections that drive growth and loyalty.

The Value of Customer Relationships

Before we explore the strategies, it's essential to understand why strong customer relationships are invaluable:

1. Repeat Business

Happy customers are more likely to return and make repeat purchases. A solid customer base provides a stable source of revenue.

2. Referrals

Satisfied customers often become brand advocates. They recommend your business to friends, family, and colleagues, helping you acquire new customers through word-of-mouth marketing.

3. Feedback and Improvement

Close customer relationships provide valuable feedback. Customer input can guide product improvements, service enhancements, and business growth strategies.

4. Brand Loyalty

Customers who feel valued and appreciated are likelier to remain loyal to your brand, even in the face of competitive alternatives.

Customer Relationship Building Strategies

Let's explore proven strategies to build and maintain strong customer relationships:

1. Personalize Your Interactions

Take the time to understand your customers individually. Address them by name, acknowledge their preferences, and tailor your communication to their needs.

2. Deliver Exceptional Customer Service

Exceptional service goes beyond satisfying basic needs. Aim to exceed customer expectations at every touchpoint, resolving issues promptly and demonstrating genuine care.

3. Engage on Social Media

Active engagement on social media allows you to connect with customers on a personal level. Respond promptly to comments, messages, and feedback, fostering a sense of community.

4. Create Loyalty Programs

Implement loyalty programs that reward repeat customers. Offer discounts, exclusive access, or special perks to incentivize ongoing engagement.

5. Seek Feedback

Regularly solicit customer feedback through surveys, reviews, and direct inquiries. Use this feedback to improve your products, services, and overall customer experience.

6. Send Personalized Thank-You Notes

Show appreciation by sending handwritten thank-you notes or personalized emails after purchases. Express your gratitude and inquire about their experience.

7. Provide Educational Content

Share valuable content that educates and informs your customers. Offer how-to guides, tips, and resources related to your products or industry.

8. Offer Exceptional Value

Consistently deliver high-quality products or services that provide tangible value to your customers. Strive to meet their needs and solve their problems effectively.

9. Host Customer Appreciation Events

Organize events or webinars specifically for your customers. These gatherings can foster a sense of belonging and allow you to connect more deeply.

10. Create a Customer Community

Build an online community or forum where customers can connect. Facilitate discussions and encourage the sharing of experiences and advice.

11. Address Problems Gracefully

Mistakes happen, but how you handle them can define your customer relationships. Acknowledge errors promptly, apologize sincerely, and resolve issues with integrity.

12. Stay Consistent

Consistency in your interactions, messaging, and branding helps build trust over time. Customers appreciate knowing what to expect.

13. Surprise and Delight

Occasionally, surprise your customers with unexpected gestures, like freebies, exclusive offers, or personalized recommendations.

14. Implement a Customer Relationship Management (CRM) System

A CRM system organizes and manages customer

information, interactions, and preferences. A well-structured CRM helps you provide more personalized service.

15. Show Empathy

Demonstrate empathy by understanding and empathizing with your customers' challenges and needs. Show that you genuinely care about their well-being.

16. Offer Exclusive VIP Benefits

Create an exclusive VIP program for your most loyal customers. Please provide them access to premium content, early product releases, or personalized services.

17. Celebrate Milestones

Acknowledge and celebrate your customers' milestones, whether a birthday, anniversary or achievement related to your products or services.

18. Follow Up Regularly

Maintain regular communication with your customers beyond the initial purchase. Check-in, offer support and provide valuable insights or resources.

19. Implement a Referral Program

Encourage referrals by implementing a program that rewards customers for bringing in new business.

20. Show Transparency

Be open and transparent with your customers. To build trust, share behind-the-scenes insights, product development updates, and company news.

Measuring Customer Relationships

To gauge the effectiveness of your customer relationship-building efforts, track key metrics such as customer satisfaction scores, Net Promoter Score (NPS), customer retention rates, and referral rates. Regularly assess these metrics to refine your strategies and ensure your relationships thrive.

Conclusion

Cultivating strong customer relationships is an ongoing process that pays dividends through repeat business, referrals, and brand loyalty. By personalizing interactions, delivering exceptional service, seeking feedback, and consistently providing value, you can create deep connections with your customers that withstand the test of time.

Remember that customer relationships are built on trust and authenticity. As you implement these strategies, stay committed to creating meaningful connections, addressing challenges gracefully, and fostering a community of loyal customers who support your business and champion it to others.

CHAPTER 10. SCALING UP WITH PROFITS

Strategies for Growing Your Business as Your Profits Increase

In your entrepreneurial journey from $100 to a profitable business, the ultimate goal is to make a profit and achieve sustainable growth. As your business becomes more profitable, you'll face the exciting challenge of scaling up. This chapter explores strategies for effectively expanding your business while maximizing the gains from your hard-earned profits.

The Journey to Profitability

Before we dive into the strategies for scaling up, it's essential to acknowledge the significance of reaching profitability:

1. Stability

Profitability provides a stable financial foundation, allowing you to cover operating costs, pay employees, and invest in growth.

2. Reinvestment

Profits offer the opportunity to reinvest in your business by expanding your product line, entering new markets, or enhancing your operations.

3. Attracting Investors

A profitable business is more appealing to investors, increasing your chances of securing additional funding for growth.

4. Long-Term Viability

Sustained profitability is a crucial indicator of your business's long-term viability and potential for success.

Scaling Up: Challenges and Opportunities

Scaling comes with a unique set of challenges and opportunities. Here are some common considerations:

1. Resource Allocation

Decide how to allocate your profits to reinvest in the business.

2. Market Expansion

Evaluate whether it's time to enter new markets, expand regionally or internationally, or diversify your customer base.

3. Operational Efficiency

Streamline operations to handle increased demand efficiently. Focus on optimizing processes and workflows.

4. Talent Acquisition

Consider hiring additional talent to support growth,

whether it's in sales, marketing, production, or other critical areas.

Strategies for Scaling Up with Profits

Here are proven strategies for scaling up your profitable business:

1. Strategic Planning

Develop a clear growth strategy that aligns with your profitability goals. Identify target markets, assess competition, and define key performance indicators (KPIs).

2. Invest in Marketing

Allocate a portion of your profits to marketing and advertising efforts. Expand your reach, refine your messaging, and reach new customer segments.

3. Product Expansion

Consider diversifying your product or service offerings. Analyze customer needs and market trends to identify expansion opportunities.

4. Geographic Expansion

Explore new geographic markets or regions where your offerings can thrive. Conduct market research to ensure your expansion efforts are well-informed.

5. E-commerce and Online Sales

Enhance your online presence and e-commerce

capabilities to reach a broader audience and facilitate growth in the digital landscape.

6. Strategic Partnerships

Collaborate with complementary businesses or industry partners to expand your customer base and offer bundled solutions.

7. Customer Retention

Focus on retaining existing customers as you scale.

8. Technology Investment

Leverage technology to streamline operations, improve customer experiences, and gain a competitive edge.

9. Financial Management

Maintain a keen eye on financial management. Monitor cash flow, control expenses, and allocate resources wisely.

10. Talent Development

Invest in employee training and development to build a capable and motivated team to support your growth.

11. Customer Feedback

Gather and analyze customer feedback to refine your products or services and adapt to changing market needs.

12. Scalable Systems

Implement scalable systems and processes that can handle increased demand without sacrificing quality.

13. Data-Driven Decision-Making

Leverage data analytics to make informed decisions. Use data to identify trends, customer behavior, and areas for improvement.

14. Risk Management

Assess and mitigate risks associated with growth, such as market volatility or increased competition.

15. Long-Term Vision

Maintain a long-term vision for your business. Avoid making short-sighted decisions that may compromise your profitability in the future.

Measuring Growth

To gauge the success of your scaling efforts, track essential metrics:

1. Revenue Growth

Monitor your revenue growth rate as a critical indicator of your business's expansion.

2. Customer Acquisition Costs (CAC)

Analyze how much it costs to acquire each new customer and assess its sustainability.

3. Customer Lifetime Value (CLV)

Calculate the CLV to understand the long-term value of your customer relationships.

4. Return on Investment (ROI)

Evaluate the return on your investment in marketing, technology, and other growth-related expenses.

5. Market Share

Assess your market share in your industry or niche to gauge your competitive position.

6. Customer Satisfaction

Continuously measure customer satisfaction and loyalty to ensure growth efforts enhance the customer experience.

Conclusion

Scaling up with profits is a thrilling phase in your business journey. As your profitability increases, it's essential to approach growth strategically, leveraging your earnings to expand intelligently and sustainably. By implementing a well-defined growth strategy, investing in marketing, diversifying products or services, and fostering a culture of innovation and adaptability, you can achieve remarkable growth without compromising the profitability you've worked so hard to attain.

Remember that scaling is not a one-time event but an ongoing process. Continuously reassess your strategies, adapt to market changes, and remain agile to seize new opportunities. With the right mindset and a strategic approach, your business can thrive and evolve, reaching new heights of success.

CHAPTER 11. OVERCOMING COMMON CHALLENGES

Solutions for Hurdles Faced by Low-Budget Startups

You'll likely encounter many common challenges in your journey, from a modest budget to building a profitable business. This chapter explores practical solutions for overcoming these hurdles. It offers guidance on navigating situations where people may doubt your ideas or where your network, including family and friends, may not provide immediate support.

The Resilience of Low-Budget Startups

Before we delve into specific challenges and solutions, it's essential to acknowledge the resilience and determination that characterize low-budget startups:

1. Resourcefulness

Low-budget startups often excel at making the most of what they have finding creative solutions to obstacles.

2. Adaptability

Starting with limited resources requires adaptability. Entrepreneurs learn to pivot when necessary and seize new opportunities.

3. Perseverance

Persistence in the face of challenges is a defining trait. Low-budget entrepreneurs are driven to prove that their ideas can succeed.

4. Confidence

Despite skepticism from others, they maintain confidence in their vision, knowing that innovation can triumph over budget constraints.

Common Challenges and Solutions

Challenge 1: Naysayers and Doubters

Solution: Embrace Constructive Criticism

Facing skepticism and doubters is typical for any new business, especially those with limited budgets. Instead of being discouraged, view criticism as an opportunity to refine your ideas. Seek feedback from mentors, advisors, and potential customers. Constructive criticism can help you make necessary improvements.

Challenge 2: Competition and Similar Alternatives

Solution: Focus on Unique Value

In a competitive market, there may be similar offerings. To stand out, emphasize your product or service's unique value proposition. Highlight what differentiates you-better quality, exceptional customer service, or a more personalized approach.

Challenge 3: Lack of Support from Family and Friends

Solution: Build an External Support Network

While family and friends might need more time to understand and support your entrepreneurial journey, building an external support network is crucial. Seek out mentors, join entrepreneurship communities, and attend networking events. Surround yourself with individuals who share your passion and can provide valuable guidance and encouragement.

Challenge 4: Limited Marketing Budget

Solution: Harness Digital Marketing

Low-budget businesses can leverage digital marketing channels like social media, content marketing, and email campaigns. These platforms offer cost-effective ways to reach your target audience and build brand awareness. Invest time learning digital marketing strategies or consider outsourcing to experts if your budget allows.

Challenge 5: Financial Constraints

Solution: Prioritize Bootstrapping

Bootstrapping involves self-funding your business with the resources you have. It's a common approach for low-budget startups. Carefully manage your expenses, reinvest profits, and explore lean business practices to minimize financial strain.

Challenge 6: Scaling with Limited Resources

Solution: Focus on Sustainable Growth

Scaling a business with limited resources requires a measured approach. Prioritize sustainable growth over rapid expansion. Set achievable milestones, gradually reinvest profits, and explore partnerships to help you scale without significant upfront costs.

Challenge 7: Fear of Failure

Solution: Embrace Failure as a Learning Opportunity

Fear of failure can be paralyzing, but viewing failure as a valuable learning experience is essential. Many successful entrepreneurs faced setbacks and failures before achieving their goals. Each failure provides insights that can guide you toward success.

Challenge 8: Balancing Work and Personal Life

Solution: Create Boundaries

Running a startup can be all-consuming, but it's crucial to maintain a balance between work and personal life. Set clear boundaries and allocate time for relaxation and spending with loved ones. A balanced life can contribute to better decision-making and overall well-being.

Challenge 9: Managing Stress and Burnout

Solution: Practice Self-Care

The entrepreneurial journey can be stressful. Regularly practice self-care, including exercise, meditation, or hobbies, to manage stress and prevent burnout. A refreshed mind is more creative and resilient.

Challenge 10: Adapting to Market Changes

Solution: Stay Agile

Markets can change rapidly. Low-budget startups should remain agile, ready to pivot and adapt to evolving trends. Regularly assess market conditions and be open to adjusting your business strategy.

The Power of Resilience and Determination

Remember that resilience and determination are your greatest assets throughout your entrepreneurial journey. Challenges are inevitable, but your ability to adapt, learn, and persist will ultimately determine your success. When others doubt your vision, use it as motivation to prove them wrong. When your resources are limited, rely on your resourcefulness to find solutions.

Conclusion

Overcoming common challenges is integral to the entrepreneurial journey, especially for startups with limited budgets. Embracing criticism, finding your unique value, seeking external support, mastering digital marketing, adopting sustainable growth practices, viewing failure as a learning opportunity, and addressing work-life balance and stress management can empower you to surmount hurdles and thrive.

As you navigate these challenges, remember that overcoming every obstacle strengthens your business acumen and builds resilience. Embrace your journey with confidence, knowing that your determination and innovative thinking will carry you toward building a profitable business.

CHAPTER 12: BUILDING A SUSTAINABLE BUSINESS

Tips for Ensuring Long-Term Success and Stability

As you progress from a small-budget startup to a profitable business, focusing on building a sustainable enterprise that can withstand challenges and thrive in the long run is essential. This chapter explores key strategies and tips for achieving long-term success and stability.

The Importance of Sustainability

Building a sustainable business means more than just generating short-term profits. It involves creating a solid foundation and a resilient framework that can adapt to changing market conditions, economic fluctuations, and unforeseen obstacles. Here are some core principles to consider:

1. Profitability vs. Sustainability

While profitability is crucial, it should not come at the expense of sustainability. Sustainable businesses prioritize long-term viability over quick gains.

2. Triple Bottom Line

Consider the triple bottom line approach, which focuses on three key aspects: economic, social, and environmental. Successful businesses aim to make a positive impact in all these areas.

3. Adaptability

Sustainable businesses are adaptable. They can pivot, adjust their strategies, and innovate when necessary to remain relevant and competitive.

Tips for Building a Sustainable Business

1. Define Your Mission and Values

A clear mission and values guide your business decisions and shape your company culture. They also resonate with customers who share your values.

2. Develop a Solid Business Plan

A well-crafted business plan outlines your goals, strategies, financial projections, and growth plans. Continually revisit and revise it to reflect changes in your business environment.

3. Build Strong Relationships

Nurturing relationships with customers, suppliers, partners, and employees is vital. Good relationships foster loyalty and open doors to new opportunities.

4. Invest in Your Team

Your employees are your greatest asset. Provide training, create a positive work environment, and offer opportunities for growth and advancement.

5. Innovate and Stay Relevant

Stay ahead of the curve by continually innovating. Monitor industry trends, seek customer feedback, and adapt your products or services to meet evolving needs.

6. Manage Finances Wisely

Maintaining a healthy cash flow and controlling expenses are critical to long-term success. Implement robust financial management practices.

7. Diversify Revenue Streams

Relying on a single source of revenue can be risky. Explore opportunities to diversify your income streams, which can provide stability during economic downturns.

8. Embrace Sustainability Practices

Incorporate sustainable practices into your operations. This can include reducing waste, conserving energy, and making eco-friendly choices.

9. Stay Committed to Quality

Quality products or services build trust with customers and reduce costly issues down the road. Make quality a core part of your brand.

10. Monitor and Measure

Use key performance indicators (KPIs) to track your progress. Regularly review data and adapt your strategies based on insights.

11. Plan for Contingencies

Prepare for unexpected challenges by having a contingency plan in place. This can include financial reserves and crisis management strategies.

12. Seek Continuous Improvement

Strive for continuous improvement in all aspects of your business. Encourage feedback from employees and customers to identify areas for growth.

13. Give Back to the Community

Contributing to your community enhances your brand's reputation and fosters goodwill and a sense of purpose.

The Journey to Long-Term Success

Building a sustainable business is a journey that requires dedication, adaptability, and a commitment to making a positive impact. It's not solely about financial gains but about leaving a lasting legacy and contributing positively to the world.

As you continue on your entrepreneurial path, remember that sustainability is not a destination but an ongoing pursuit. Embrace the principles discussed in this chapter, and let them guide your decisions as you work toward long-term success and stability.

Conclusion

This chapter explored the importance of building

a sustainable business and provided tips for achieving long-term success and stability. Remember that sustainability encompasses economic, social, and environmental aspects, a journey that requires continuous effort and dedication.

By defining your mission, investing in your team, managing finances wisely, and staying committed to quality, you can create a business that thrives financially and positively impacts the world. As you embark on this journey, keep sustainability principles at the forefront of your business decisions, and you'll be well on your way to building a lasting and meaningful enterprise.

CHAPTER 13: FINANCIAL MANAGEMENT FOR A $100 HUSTLE

Tips and Ideas to Make the Most of Your Limited Budget

Starting a business with just $100 requires precise financial management. This chapter explores essential tips and ideas to optimize your financial resources, even when your budget is minimal.

The Significance of Financial Management

With a limited budget, financial management becomes your lifeline. It's about tracking expenses and strategically using every dollar to drive growth. Here's why it matters:

1. Survival and Growth: Effective financial management is essential for survival and future growth.

2. Resource Allocation: It helps you allocate your limited funds where they'll have the most significant impact on your business.

3. Risk Mitigation: Proper management helps identify and mitigate financial risks, reducing the chances of unexpected setbacks.

4. Informed Decisions: It provides data for making informed decisions about pricing, investments, and other critical aspects.

Strategies for $100 Startups

1. Create a Bare-Bones Budget

Develop a minimal budget that covers only essential expenses. Focus on what you need to get started.

2. Bootstrapping All the Way

Embrace the bootstrapping mindset. Avoid taking on debt or significant expenses early on. Rely on your resources and creativity.

3. Free and Low-Cost Tools

Utilize free and low-cost tools for essential tasks like website building, social media management, and communication.

4. DIY Marketing

Be your marketer. Use free social media platforms, content marketing, and word-of-mouth to spread the word about your business.

5. Lean Operations

Keep overhead costs to a minimum. Operate from a home office, share resources, and only hire when necessary.

6. Frugal Advertising

If you need advertising, focus on cost-effective methods like targeted online ads or leveraging local partnerships.

7. Customer-Funded Growth

Let your customers fund your growth. Offer pre-sales or crowdfunding campaigns to generate revenue.

8. Continuous Learning

Invest in your knowledge and skills. Learn how to manage your finances effectively and maximize your limited resources.

Conclusion

Starting a business with just $100 requires careful financial management. Creating a minimalist budget, embracing bootstrapping, using free and low-cost tools, and frugal advertising are vital strategies for success. Remember that continuous learning and a resourceful mindset will be your greatest assets.

As you implement these tips and ideas tailored to your limited budget, you'll be better equipped to navigate the financial challenges and maximize your resources to grow your $100 startup.

Throughout this chapter, we've explored essential tips and ideas for managing your limited budget effectively. Now, let's recap the key takeaways and encourage you on your unique entrepreneurial path:

1. The Power of Precision:

• Begin by creating a bare-bones budget that covers only the essentials.

• Prioritize spending on what's necessary to get your business off the ground.

2. Embrace Bootstrapping:

• The bootstrapping mindset will be your greatest ally. Avoid taking on debt or unnecessary expenses.
• Rely on your resourcefulness and creativity to maximize what you have.

3. Leverage Free and Low-Cost Tools:

• Explore the free and low-cost tools for essential tasks like website development, social media management, and communication.
• Harness these resources to operate efficiently without breaking the bank.

4. Become Your Marketer:

• Marketing doesn't have to be expensive. Embrace do-it-yourself marketing strategies, utilizing social media, content marketing, and word-of-mouth to promote your business.

5. Run a Lean Operation:

• Keep your overhead costs minimal. Consider operating from a home office, sharing resources, and only hiring when necessary.
• Every dollar saved is a dollar that can be reinvested into your business's growth.

6. Frugal Advertising:

• If advertising is necessary, focus on cost-effective methods such as targeted online ads or partnerships within your local community.

7. Engage in Customer-Funded Growth:

• Your customers can become your biggest supporters. Consider offering pre-sales or crowdfunding campaigns to generate revenue and fuel your growth.

8. Continuous Learning:

• Invest in your knowledge and skills. The more you learn about financial management and resource optimization, the better you'll navigate the challenges ahead.

As you embark on your journey with a $100 startup, remember that your determination, resilience, and adaptability will be your greatest assets. You are part of a community of entrepreneurs who have transformed humble beginnings into successful businesses.

While the road ahead may have twists and turns, it's also filled with opportunities for growth and innovation. Stay focused on your goals, remain open to learning, and embrace the entrepreneurial spirit that drives you forward.

Your journey is unique, and your $100 hustle has the potential to become something extraordinary. By applying the principles and strategies outlined in this chapter, you take the first steps toward turning your vision into reality. As you navigate the challenges and celebrate the successes, remember that every small win brings you closer to your ultimate destination.

The path of entrepreneurship is not always easy, but it's a path that promises fulfillment, independence, and the opportunity to create something remarkable. Your $100 hustle is not just a venture; it's an adventure, and we wish you every success as you embark on this exciting journey.

Chapter 14: Turning Vision into Profit

Congratulations on completing "The $100 Hustle Blueprint for a Profitable Business!" You've embarked on a journey from humble beginnings to entrepreneurship, armed with determination, creativity, and a budget of $100. As this book ends, let's recap the vital lessons and set your course for success.

1. Starting Small, Dreaming Big:

• You've learned that a small budget is not a barrier but a creative catalyst.
• Your dreams have no limits; they only require resourcefulness and resilience.

2. The Power of Innovation:

• Innovation is your ally; it allows you to find unique solutions on a tight budget.
• Don't be afraid to challenge conventions and explore uncharted territories.

3. Listening to Your Market:

• Your audience is your compass; listen to their needs and adapt your offerings.
• Market research can uncover valuable insights even on a shoestring budget.

4. Planning for Success:

• A lean business plan tailored to your goals is your roadmap to success.
• Keep your vision clear, objectives achievable, and strategies flexible.

5. Resource Maximization:

• The art of cost-cutting is your secret weapon; optimize resources and reduce waste.
• Every dollar saved is a dollar you can invest in growth.

6. Hustling for Capital:

• Be resourceful in raising capital; consider creative funding options.
• Your determination can inspire others to support your vision.

7. DIY Branding and Marketing:

• Branding doesn't require a big budget; authenticity and passion resonate.
• Leverage cost-effective marketing techniques to spread the word.

8. Building Customer Relationships:

• Cultivate strong bonds with your customers; they are

your best advocates.
• Repeat business and referrals are the lifeblood of your venture.

9. Navigating Challenges:

• Challenges are part of the journey; view them as growth opportunities.
• Overcome obstacles with creativity, persistence, and a positive mindset.

10. Sustainability and Longevity:

- Your business is built for the long haul; focus on sustainability.
- Continuously adapt, learn, and evolve to thrive in changing landscapes.

11. Your Unique Path:

- Your journey is one-of-a-kind, filled with twists, turns, and surprises.
- Embrace the adventure of entrepreneurship, knowing that every step counts.

As you forge ahead, remember that success is not measured solely in dollars but in the impact you create, the lives you touch, and the legacy you leave. Your $100 hustle has the potential to bloom into a thriving business, and your story will inspire others to take their leaps of faith.

Stay curious, stay bold, and remain true to your vision. Keep exploring, innovating, and making a difference in the world. Your entrepreneurial spirit is a force to be reckoned with, and your journey has just begun.

Thank you for choosing "The $100 Hustle Blueprint for a Profitable Business" as your guide.

www.ingramcontent.com/pod-product-compliance
Lightning Source LLC
Chambersburg PA
CBHW072340290526
45794CB00002B/950